Bapu in My Dream

Poetry Across Time, People and Pandemic

R. P. Ghosh

ISBN 979-8-88805-372-0

Dedication

On the Seventy-Fifth Year
of my Country's Independence in 2022;
reverently I bow my head to the departed souls
of the freedom fighters who had sacrificed their
lives for the freedom of our Nation, and
I dedicate these poems to their
magnanimous memories.

Contents

Also by the Author

'Podatik' (Pedestrian) – Collection of Bengali Stories, written by the author, based on his experiences and interactions with people in India and abroad, from time to time. Published in April 2003.

'Eklavyer Noibedya' (Offerings of 'Eklavya') – Collection of Bengali Poems. Published in April 2003.

'Sukh-Sagorer Khonj' (Search for Eternal Enlightenment) – Collection of Bengali Poems. Published in April 2003.

'Beedehir Roop' (Beauty of the Bodiless) – Collection of Bengali Poems. Published in August 2006.

'Lunchita Sakuntala' (Humiliated 'Sakuntala') – Bengali Poem of a one-act play, referring to 'Sakuntala' of an Indian epic on the theme of women's oppression in human society. Published in January 2010.

'Mondakinir Achena Pakhi' (Unknown bird of 'Mandakini') – Collection of Bengali Poems.

Published in August 2010. (By 'Prativash', Kolkata, India)

'Bosonter Vorbela' (Morning of the Spring) – Collection of Bengali Poems. Published in January 2013. (By Saptarshi Prakashan, Kolkata, India.)

'Poetry Collection... And The Modhumoti Flows Quietly' – Collection of English Poems. Published in June 2016. (By Olympia Publishers, London)

'The Treasure Of Tears' – Collection of English Poems. Published in May 2018. (By Olympia Publishers, London.)

'Polasher Rupokar' (Creator of 'Polash' flower, the flame of the forest) – Collection of Bengali Poems. Published in October 2018. (By Saptarshi Prakashan, Kolkata, India)

'Beloved Oblivion' – Collection of English Poems. Published in September 2020. (By Olympia Publishers, London.)

'Bhopal Gas Tragedy' – Collection of English Poems. To be published in 2022. (By Blue Rose Publishers, New Delhi, India.)

Acknowledgments

Life and Nature have always acted on me as boons of fortune. I am grateful for their abundant blessings. Apart from their almightiness, I feel lucky to have a wide circle of patrons, readers, and well-wishers, who remember me regularly, honour, and review my creative and literary talents and outputs, thereby encouraging my efforts in a positive mood, to guide me with the right perspective all the time.

I am always eager to receive the comments, criticisms, and reactions of readers and poetry-lovers, as I believe, these will pave the direction towards perfection.

I am grateful to the entire team of Notion Press Media Private Limited, who have extended their whole-hearted generosity and support to publish this book of poems, thereby providing me with an opportunity to reach a wider spectrum of readers, reviewers, critics, and patrons as well, beyond my expectations, crossing borders and barriers.

I acknowledge the support and assistance of the media, as well.

My thanks to everyone involved in the process of marketing the book worldwide, directly or indirectly.

Truly yours,
R. P. Ghosh.
Mobile & WhatsApp:+91 9871168861.
Email: ghoshr77@yahoo.in

Date: 15th August 2022.
Kolkata-70009, India.

One Lonely Lady

One popular leader is now addressing a meeting
to appeal to general people for a progressive society
by adopting necessary actions; in order to mobilise
the process of uplifting females, equal to males.

Assembled public; with great enthusiasm, appreciate
the local leader's statement and cheer with clapping.
Immediately from the crowd, one lady interacts
in her nervous and trembling voice—
"Dear Sir! Before the adoption of corrective measures;
it is absolutely necessary to change natural habits
of the male genders of our society."

The curious audience loudly
asks about the identity of the lady.

In response; the lady gently informs the crowd,
—I am a female member of a middle-class family
in your neighbourhood, living in this suburban town.
My ancestors were earlier living in
the western province of the united union.
After the partition of this country;
during Independence, along with my parents

and relatives, at an early age, I had to leave
our original hometown and became a refugee
to migrate here to this present address.
I got my education from a local school and college.
To the irony of my fate; after completion
of my education, I was married to a prospective
young handsome groom, who had settled abroad.
But, shortly after the marriage, I was deserted
by my husband, and I became a lonely lady!

The lady continued—
After completion of the marriage ceremony; and
enjoying the honey-moon together; my husband
left our home town, and went back to the country,
where he was posted for his job originally.
Before saying goodbye to me;
lovingly he promised me that he would arrange
the necessary visa and other documents for me
to travel to that country for our reunion.
He convinced me that
the process would take considerable time.

I believed him and allowed him to leave me
under the care of my elderly parents, with the hope
of shaping the reality of having my own happy home.
The months passed, one by one.
But I never received the visa and travel documents.
It became an uphill task for me to cross the hurdles;
one after another to convince my all well-wishers.

Ultimately, via media, the situation became clear.
I am deprived of my fortune due to the unsupportive
and cheating behaviour of my non-resident husband,
as he already had a family there and was not willing
to get me to the country he was living in.
For no fault of mine, my fortune
crumbled at such a young age.

My neighbours, irrespective of age, faith, and gender
cursed me and my character without a valid reason.
Most of them conveniently concluded that,
my loose character would have been the reason
for his refusal to arrange my visa and travel documents.

It was my fate most tragic; neither did that man agree
to accept me as his wife, nor did he divorce me legally.
Thereby; he did not allow me to settle my life in the future.

As days passed on; even my parents started feeling
that I was becoming a liability.
In their old age, they expected to be looked after
by their children since their finances were low
and their health was ailing.
Finding no other way to survive; based on my
educational qualification, I had to look for a suitable job.
Ultimately, I was selected for a job in a mercantile firm,
thereby, getting an opportunity to earn my bread and
butter.

It became my daily routine to leave home in the
morning,
and return in the evening after attending my office
work.
My curious neighbours, irrespective of gender
became suspicious about my movements and started
taunting me, even complaining to my parents
about my outlook, nature, and above all, my character.
They were even jealous of my independent behaviour.
Some of them even passed silly and vulgar remarks.
On these aspects; irrespective of age, cast, creed,
and gender, all of them were very liberal.
I feel ashamed to tell you the fact that
members of both genders tried hard to lure me
into immoral activities and heinous social offences.

Alas! This is the society I live in, where both
men and women claim their equal rights rationally
to accuse or blame me without having solid ground.
But, at the time of my distress, none of them came
forward to extend their support, help, and cooperation.
They turned miserly and tightfisted to praise my
perseverance and capacity to face odd situations.

Wholeheartedly; I pray for that day when nature
and attitude of the human beings will be
transformed and mobilised towards positivity.

Being a member of the feminine gender of this society,
I never wanted to be self-reliant and independent.
I had the option of fulfilling my ambition of having
a family of my own, with my husband and to become
a mother, and to live peacefully with dignity and
not to be deprived of availing the facilities, due to
the gender inequality that prevails in human society.

Oh, my dear judicious and far-sighted leader!
The people, who are inclined and interested
to mobilise themselves for a progressive and
dynamic gender-equal society, please vow
to bring a change in the behaviour and attitude
of both genders, male and female.

Before going ahead with the implementation
of your action; please have a look at my sufferings,
that I have come across in my life, time to time.
Please try to manifest the purity and perfection
already in man of both the genders, male and female.

13 May, 2018

The Thirsty Skylarks

On the advice of the Monsoon season;
the month of July forwarded advance information,
indicating its ensuing arrival, to end a hot
and dry spell from Nature.

Eventually, the thirsty Skylarks have become
highly delighted to greet and welcome
the Monsoon season.
Stretching their tiny wings; the jolly birds fly
in the sky, following each other in circular form
in the shape of a garland, to honour the Monsoon
without caution.

A flock of naughty Martins, the house-mynas;
well-known for their quarrelsome behaviour,
feel irritated with Skylarks' unruly flying style
and scold them to behave properly.

But the Skylarks hardly bother; rather reply,
— Nearly a year is about to be over, since then
we have not been able to quench our thirst
up to the level of our satisfaction.
The sky has been reluctant to listen to our

earnest appeal so far.
Alternatively, nobody has taken over
the responsibility, even for a while, to arrange
a few raindrops for us.

Very shortly, we shall be highly delighted
and obliged to meet the much-awaited
Monsoon season, our most beloved.
The patches of dark clouds are moving
around the sky, to obey the wind's direction.
We are anxious to meet each other,
and to have a pleasant bath together
in her holy and auspicious presence.

The Peacocks and Peahens, posing in their usual
dancing postures, affirm support to the Skylarks,
— The raindrops will create the wedding beds
for togetherness of thirsty Skylarks.
We will also participate in the dancing carnival,
while expanding our colourful plumage
in circular motifs, like fans, to glorify the event.
We are sure Nature will also not lag behind.

She will transform the flora all around
into a bright and lively sap-green.

19 August, 2018

Poverty—My Loving Step-Mother

All my relations, near and dear,
agreed upon the fact—
Although my mother had given me birth,
'Poverty', as my step-mother, brought me up
with her love and care.

Hostile situations in my childhood days;
like many others, turned me into a homeless refugee.
With the grace of my step-mother 'Poverty',
I got the feeling of hard soil under my feet.

In the initial stage; practising her noble teachings
paved the avenues of meagre livelihood
to get rid of the thirst and hunger that had
ultimately developed the sustaining capacity.
Thereby growing the perseverance within me
as an individual.

Based on her kind advice and proper attention,
I gathered the courage and stamina to bear the
sufferings that had cropped up from the roughness
of grits and pebbles spread over the Earth's surface.
Her guidance afforded me the capacity for tolerance,

and the power of confrontation against the odds
in every sphere of my life, year after year.

As 'Time' the great crawled on,
under her guidance, I learnt to draw the lines
of ambitious traits on the back-drop of
unaccounted odds, thereby, achieving power
of apperception, that perfected my vision
to appreciate the beauty of the vast greenery,
where the variety of birds nestle and rehearse
the tunes of eternity.
Further activating the capacity to visualise
the sacred line of the earthly horizon where the sky
comes down with a desire for togetherness.
And the breeze blows the flow of cordiality all over.

Better late than never; my step-mother 'Poverty'
taught me hymns to praise the goddess of 'Wealth'
and also the goddess of 'Learning' that combined
both— the intellect and sense of creativity within me.
In due course, it enlightened me
to attain the fulfilment of life, love, and affection
of my associates and neighbours around me.

The Poverty; my beloved step-mother!
Humbly I bow my head at your holy feet
as a mark of gratitude till my last breath.

27 August, 2018

Before the Indoctrination

All day long; since morning, I was busy playing
dirty games with my naughty playmates.
Without caring regular system; I followed many tricks
not to lose the games, but to win every time.
Due to my fickle mind; I have not been able to request
my mother to clean my dirty face before she desires
to cuddle me on her affectionate lap.

Revered Preceptor! Similarly,
you first purify my body and mind thoroughly,
before you decide to indoctrinate me passionately.
Otherwise; your noble effort might turn out to be futile.
It would be considered an untimely
and unwise effort on your part.

Very well you know; all the evils—
like jealousy, cheating and greediness are well-settled
at the core of my heart and mind.
To win wealth without perseverance and to conspire
for unauthorised encroachment on other's right
at an opportune moment, my consciousness does not
feel guilty even for a single moment.

Dressed in neat and clean apparel always I pretend
to be honest and righteous before social dignitaries.
I represent myself as judicious to declare the verdict
of penalties on others' offences.
Do these practices not reflect my cleverness,
or degradation of human value and status?

I think my mind is unfit yet to be baptised
in any of the solace reforms for purification.
Let me forgo all my egos, jealousy, and desire
of acquiring power and sovereignty.
Let me live a simple life, but make rich by heart.
Let me grow like a lotus bud within the dirt.

Afflict me to taste my inherent demerits and enjoy
the qualities of tolerance and endurance.
Shedding my tears for the distressed and sufferers;
I shall take a holy dip of purification of my mind.
Perhaps; only then, I shall be able for indoctrination.

06 September, 2018

A Few Unfulfilled Desires

Irrespective of my willingness
I may expect the final call at any moment.
But I have a few desires yet to be fulfilled.
Otherwise, my candidature may not be
considered for an elevation.

Not even once I stepped inside the corridor
of the Parliament House or Assembly Building.
Though I took around the surroundings
several times of these important locations,
as a tourist guide.

I have visited many prominent sacred and
religious places around the world.
But I have yet to pay a visit to the prostitutes.
Though their lives are reflected and covered
as prominent characters in many kinds of literature.
I have come across the lanes and bylanes
of their residential locations on many occasions.

Yes, it is directed in a few religious edicts that,
the soil of their residential localities is considered
holy and auspicious.

Even a little quantity of soil claims mandatory
to make the idol of the goddess before worshipping.

I have yet to get into a jail or prison
for committing any crime or offence
in the eyes of civil laws in practice.

Due to lack of these important experiences;
down to the Earth, I cannot claim myself
as perfect and suitable for an elevation.
Pardon me please if I have pinned sentiments
of all the noble human beings in our society.

11 September, 2018

Melodrama of the Malady

Since childhood, I have taken 'Life'
into confidence as my trustworthy companion,
though the Malady has silently acted as
one of my close associates.

Day by day I also witnessed the fact that
the Malady very often exerts her massive
influencing role and dominating power
on all life-beings, throughout the world.
'Life' then quietly observes the
consequences as a silent spectator.

Each day, while swinging between the quibbles
of these two, I try hard to proceed with all my
sincerity towards the fulfilment of my aspirations.

Often, while noticing my close intimacy
with the Malady, the 'Life' in his usual
casual mood cautions me with a warning—
Dear! It is neither praiseworthy,
nor, tolerable on your part at all.

But, 'Life' fails to realise my helplessness!
I do not really know the process; of how to
refuse undue favour from the witty Malady,
as she appears in disguise at any moment,
all of a sudden, as an unbidden guest, though
her presence is not willingly solicited for.

Having no other option to offer; now
pointing her index finger towards me,
the rigid and shrewd Malady threatens—
In the end; only she would stand
in a position to direct and guide me,
how to reach the final destination,
the ultimate goal towards salvation.
The 'Life' then will obviously observe silence.
Even he will not be seen anywhere nearby
to respond to your ardent call in distress.

21 September, 2018

Pacing with the Optimism

After the darkened night; as the Sun rises,
the dawn appears delightfully, like a toddler.
During the day, I venture out everywhere
to grab the opportunity of something substantial.
But all in vain, I retain ultimately only the hope
in my mind, nothing else.

Every moment speeds on to make an hour.
Similarly, hours pass on silently to count the day.
Days follow to form the month, and the months
run towards the years, then to decades, and so on.
Nevertheless, the outcome remains nil.
The unfulfilled desire; as the optimism does not
keep pace with reality on practical terms.

At this moment, the mind consoles—
By any chance, if you earn enormous wealth,
where you will store them in safe custody
to ensure secured possession for future needs,
as you do not have even a shed on your head!
Even if you achieve fame through your talent,
that will surely make you proud and arrogant.
The reactions thereon; will continuously pinch

your tender heart as you are not refined.
Thereby; it will make you uncomfortable.

Keeping in view all these consequences,
the time tasted proverb moves mouth to mouth
beyond centuries—
Optimism begets nothing; unless and until
it keeps pace with the ground reality!

25 September, 2018

Love Tryst of the Stars

To overcome loneliness; I get up early
and proceed towards a small courtyard
surrounded with green foliage all around.
Seasonal flowers, mainly the 'Night Jasmine'
are in full bloom, while spreading the essence
to adorn the auspicious season of Autumn.
Cool air is busy in flowing the holy message
of the festive season all over Nature.

The stars twinkle in the sky smilingly,
and beckon me with love signs for togetherness.
Lovingly, they convey,
— Dear! A few minutes onward, all the birds
will fly away from their nests in
different directions to their destinations.
— The beloved Poet!
Do not miss this is high time to seek their
good gestures, and request them to fly you
on their wide wings and bring near to us
for our amorous hugs as a mark of cordial
relationship of our togetherness.
— Dear! Do not delay further; otherwise
the jealous Sun will surely spoil our plan.

Not to allow our togetherness without any
interference, he will surely enlighten the sky.
We will miss our long-awaited love tryst,
since the solar system has already enforced
the restriction on our close relationship
on the Earth's surface, beyond the horizon.
— Perhaps, you have not yet forgotten the fact.
The number of times in the past; you accused
the mighty Sun in the lyrics of your poetry
for his indecent and obscene behaviour towards
his loyal devotee –'Kunti', innocent virgin-girl
of the Indian epic, the 'Mahabharata'.

Ultimately, 'Kunti' had to bear the odds in her life,
which is known to common people today even.
Before the dawn is over, please appeal to the birds
for an early action to fulfil our desire.

02 October, 2018

The Invisible Painter & Sculptor

The floating patches of the Autumn clouds!
No, no, no— You will not be permitted
to transform yourself into rain-water;
nearly for a year, probably till the next Monsoon.

Both of us, you and I shall not get a chance
to meet each other.
But take it granted, my love tryst mind
will look forward till then.
In my leisure, with a thirsty mind, I look high
in the sky for a glance of your tender beauty
in different contours.
On mild airflow; you mould your slim figure
and shape yourself frequently in different
artistic forms and figures.

I wonder! Who is your teacher,
the invisible Painter-n-Sculptor
inspiring your creativity in every moment?
At an opportune time in the future; will you
please introduce me to that great painter, so as to

make my soul pure with the noble touch of his noble and refined gesture?

The artistic mind within me, till then, will wait for that auspicious and holy moment in silence.

04 October, 2018

This is not Slander

My faith, respect, and adoration for you—
On this point; many people, known and
unknown, unnecessarily accuse me very often.
Undoubtedly, this accusation against me is slander.
Further; those people formulate a bunch of
allegations to create a strong lobby against me.

My trust, love, and respect for you—
If these are considered criminal offences;
let your appointed bench of judges scrutinise
the allegation, and ascertain trustworthiness
of your constitutional procedure, whatsoever.
Is there any such prescribed law of punishment
in the forum against these types of offences?

My affection, devotion, and dedication to you—
If these are considered criminal offences;
I am guilty beyond doubt, and I bow my head.
Obediently I shall accept all the punishments.
I shall consider them all as your kind blessings,
as long as I live in this world.

I shall bear full faith in my heart—
In accusation of my reverence for you,
the punishment that I have been sentenced,
is my ultimate desire, infinitive joy,
supreme satisfaction of my life, nonetheless.

16 November, 2018

Charisma of Colour

While going through the learning process
I have explored and come to a conclusion
that you are ever-young and vibrant.
Your excellence is adjudged on a magical basis
combined with other tones and shades, laying
side by side, one after another.

You have always considered me as one of your
trusted companions; thereby, I have been able
to console me whenever my mind has plunged
into the confusion on the versatility of life.

Perhaps you are aware of the fact that;
you are identified by most common people
as deaf and dumb, without having any caste,
creed, and language, even faith.
I object to their concept vehemently and believe
from the core of my heart; you rather speak loudly
like an expert with an excellent vocabulary.
And that has, no doubt, enriched the heritage of
human civilisation since the stone age.

You represent 'white', which symbolises peace,
the sign of brotherhood worldwide.
You represent the 'saffron' as a sign of sacrifice
and renunciation to defraying from a lavish and
luxurious life.
You have, as well, given the noble identity of
different national flags as a sign of independence
and sovereignty, as respected worldwide.

Honourable Colour!
Side by side, you represent human society
in two definitions—Black and White!
Ultimately, the sequences had germinated
hate and apartheid indulging the discrepancy.
And the consequences; thereby, had compelled
many to turn into homeless refugees!
You even define it as a victory sign on the forehead
of some section of rulers, also as a sectarian mark
of religious faith in certain sections of society.

My dear Colour!
You represent the beauty of the invisible Almighty
spreading all over Nature; in order to differentiate
the seasons, one after another throughout the year.
During the rainy season; you offer Nature
a palate of different shades to paint a rainbow
that covers both ends of the horizon to inspire
the pee-cocks to dance on vast meadows.

In Autumn, blooming plants 'night-queen'
inspire the human mind to worship the deity.
During Spring, you inspire Nature
in a blooming spree to attract the butterflies
to kiss the flower petals of different shades.
These actions motivate the cuckoos to sing.

Further, you are a vibrant source of inspiration
flowing through the veins of all living beings.

Above all, I differentiate your most charming
spectrum, as and when, you spread yourself
in layers of different glares on a canvas, that
ultimately illustrates the image of 'Madonna',
the virgin mother Merry holding the holy child
Jesus in her arms.
Or, the Lord-Buddha as prince, child 'Gautama'
in the arms of his mother-queen 'Gautomi' in a
full-moon night at 'Kapilavastu'.
Even Lord Krishna as a naughty child
on the lap of his mother 'Yasoda' in Mathura.

20 November, 2018

Wintery Desire of the 'Night Jasmine'

During winter, the air whispers very often
to the cold-stricken flower, the 'Night Jasmine',
— Darling! Have you overheard their hints,
confidential discussions between the buds
swinging on peduncles of the 'Cotton flower'
and 'Bastard', which are widely known as
'flames of the forests' to nature lovers?

Buds have planned to cover up all of Nature
in vermilion during the Spring season;
to enhance the behaviour of all life-beings
transfusing cordiality and amity to welcome
the New Year for fulfilling their desires.

We all know, Spring—the king of all seasons
is just about to knock on our doors,
it's a matter of only a few weeks to pass on!

However, in Winter, the wintery flower—
'Night Jasmine', being crippled by the flow
of the cold wind, expects the gracious favour
from the great Sun, during dawn, to cross over

the lanes and bylanes of high-rise apartments
and reflect his shines to her green tender stems
and buds even for a while!

The noble 'Night Jasmine' humbly desires—
With the warm embarrassment of the Sun, obviously
she will regain her inherent aspiration of love
in the coming seasons, especially during Autumn.
She will also be able to offer her amiable presence
with petals, full of essence, to the mighty goddess,
while appearing on the Earth to bless devotees.

Further, her efforts will, no doubt, pave the path
of devotion and ultimate satisfaction of souls
to the countless worshipers and nature lovers.

14 January, 2019

The Sun—Another One

While following amiable and orderly behaviour among the planets and stars; including the Sun, the solar system of the Universe is moving in order without facing any kind of laps, or disorder so far, as per the human calendar.

Though, side by side, a large number of scientists, worldwide, are engaged in research day and night to achieve ultimate objectives,
— How to invent and develop the most modern
and the latest technology of nuclear fusions;
intercontinental atom bombs, which can never
be intercepted by any rival power or competitor.

Further, rumours on the same topic spread all over, from mouths to mouths, while millions of common, peace-loving people feel pity to note the fact that
— leaders worldwide are sincerely engaged
to voice the slogan of their strategic plan;
how to impose domination on others, without
having any jurisdiction, care, or responsibility.

While observing all these developments minutely;
the generous Sun above the sky cuts joke smilingly,
— Oh, the idiots down on Earth!
Mobilising the process of destruction
through nuclear explosions, you all are keen
to achieve success to rule others on this Earth.
If you are really keen on achieving success;
please plan positively to create another Sun,
which would be even more powerful and vibrant
than that of mine.
You all know, I burn myself always to enlighten
all the planets and stars throughout the Universe.
— Oh, my dear! Only then your heart and mind
will feel satisfied to become another Sun, like me.
And you will definitely consider yourself lucky
for being blessed a life of human being, which is
always considered as a supreme desire
of all life-beings on this lovely Earth!

24 January, 2019

Yamuna—The Swindled River

To get the motherly touch of the holy river, Yamuna,
often I used to visit her via the town, 'Mathura',
the famous places in the history of ancient India.
I was blessed with her grace on each occasion
during the full-moon night of each month of the year.
With satisfaction of mind, I used to enjoy
the beauty of the natural water flow of the holy river.

The long mundane period of the 'Treta' era,
during divine incarnation of Lord 'Krishna'
and his lover 'Radhika' was over long back.
The rows of flowering plants on the river-bank,
where the naughty cowherd-boy 'Krishna' had
played with his playmates, were not in existence.
Even then, the essence of the eternal love episode
used to rejuvenate in the breeze air all around,
with the symphony of clear water of the river.

One by one, the decades have crawled over.
The flow of devotees for a holy bath in the river
has decreased, and business ventures have increased.
Hardly a singer to sing devotional songs is visible.

Due to a lack of cleanliness and poor maintenance,
the river Yamuna has turned decrepit and lean.

We, the devotees are guilty of her senile health.
With the main objective of fulfilling our self-interest,
we have ignored her sacred touch for decades,
and avoided our premier duties to look after her.

Today, while sitting near the bank of narrow
and contaminated flow of the river, Yamuna,
my disheartened mind looks behind
her healthy, holy, and natural flow in the past.
The heart within me asks my crumbled mind—
Is there any provision of our expiation to get rid
of willful crimes, generations after generations?

04 February, 2019

Rehabilitation of Deities

To maintain cordial relation with the Sun;
every morning, at early dawn, I roam the lawns
near my residence.
Then, very frequently I meet my neighbours
and close associates freely without any bar.
In reciprocation, I receive their good-wishes,
even whole-hearted blessings from the elders.
I respect and revere them all as my gods.

Rows of fully grown trees; all along the roads
silently provide pollution-free air and shadows
in abundance to the passersby, even extend
shelters to the homeless and abandoned.
I notice many uncared deities of different faiths
are now abandoned on those secluded platforms.

I do not know the actual reasons for their rejection –
The deities once cordoned under many
ritual barriers; are now free from all restrictions
and cordial to each other, without any hindrance.

My secular and inherent-artistic mind believes—
above all, godly and holy feelings exist

in different forms of art, irrespective of faith.
The sense of this realisation drives me out from all
religious barriers and inspires to bring the idols
to my shabby residence with the prime objective
of preserving them as precious art collections.

Remembering my early refugee life in the past,
I console my mind with a great feeling of fulfilment—
My action is considered nothing but an act
of repetition of holy rehabilitation of gods.
My presence on the scene is only a consequence;
and nothing else!

14 February, 2019

To Please the Spring

My dear mother, Nature!
Pardon me please for not being able
to fiddle the musical instrument right in time,
while welcoming the Spring, on the eve of his
gracious appearance on this Earth's surface,
once a year.
As you are aware of the fact, at that moment,
on your prior advice, I was busy enquiring
on the blooming status of different foliage
like 'Simool', the cotton flower, and others.

Your obedient followers, all the flowers
feel obliged to be attracted
by the butterflies and hornets in this season.
At that moment, I have to convince the wind
to flow gently and create the right atmosphere
for the pollination.

In addition, I had not only to co-sponsor
the musical concert on behalf of the cuckoos,
but also to find out suitable nests for them
to lay the eggs for their motherhood,
to carry on the age-old tradition in vogue.

I had also to train and rehearse the groups
of peacocks and peahens on dancing lessons
to perform on the vast stage in the presence of
distinguished guests from hell and heaven
beyond this planet.

The plants, namely 'Polash',
commonly known as 'flames of the forests'
are equally enthused and energised
in accelerating their inherent artistic talents
for the supreme perfection on an open canvas.
They are looking forward to bag praise
from the lord of all planets, the Sun.

Even though, my appeals may not have
valid reasons to justify my absence
on this holy occasion, with all my sincerity
I beg your pardon.

15 February, 2019

Evening Prayer to the 'Nile' River

Oh, the glittering river—'Nile'!
Let me light an evening lamp to offer my prayer
to your godly presence on this earthly soil.
Not only I, but all human community worldwide
pay respect to your juvenile beauty.
People from their hearts truly believe—
you are the pioneer of human civilisation.

Further, I pay my regards to the civilians,
who were lucky enough to be obliged by your
good gesture, generation after generation.

Oh, the glittering river—'The Nile' of 'Misr' valley!
You are the main lifeline for not only one Nation,
but the entire region of the continent.
From your gentle flow; let me collect a few drops
of water on my palm, so that I may sprinkle them
on my head to purify my body, mind, and soul.
Dear! I follow the same practice, as and when,
I pay my visit to the 'Ganges', another holy river
flowing down from the Himalayan ranges.

While flowing down to the Mediterranean Sea,
please convey my regards to him, as I know,
he, among a few others, maintains the balance
between the volume of aqua and mass on the Earth.

But the glittering river—'Nile'!
How can one overlook the painful facts that,
silently you have been bearing odds for decades?
Nature changes its geographic pattern.
Accordingly, islets were formed on your river-bed
at a turning point in the flowing direction.
Instead of reviving the natural flow to taste your
level of affection towards us, and your capacity
of endurance, the islets have been commercially
exploited by constructing hotels and motels
on the pretext of the prosperity of human society.

You know— queen 'Cleopatra' is no more.
Perhaps the love tryst of her heart and soul, lying
deep under the pyramid in the desert of El-Giza,
feels anguished due to artificial changes
on her favourite river-bed, where she used to enjoy
boat-riding during the glittering full-moon night
with her near and dear and beloveds.
But history remains intact.
Human interference cannot detract from the fact.

21 February, 2019

Crowning Anniversary of Spring

Without any valid reason whatsoever,
very often I reach your address
whenever I like to get in touch with you.
In the advent of a cool breeze, on every occasion
you embrace me cordially and whisper in my ear
while briefing me on the exact date of your
wedding anniversary.
Every year, I eagerly wait for your invitation.

My dear Spring!
At this remarkable and colourful event,
to my surprise, this time I have not yet been able
to find out the gracious presence of cuckoos
anywhere in nature.
I do not know the actual reasons behind it.
Perhaps the untimely presence of an unwanted guest —
the 'Rain' might have dampened the mood
of other invitees, thereby, causing probable reason
for annoyance that had ultimately stopped
the singers from joining this holy participation.

Avoiding contrariety in weather conditions
I feel delighted to be present here

on this festive celebration.
Seasonal flowers; 'Simool', the cotton flower,
accompanied by 'Polash', widely known as
'flames of the forest', are already present here
with their treasure trove and colourful resources
to grace this occasion.

I am the only invitee present here empty-handed;
without any souvenirs, as I have nothing
to offer you on this holy celebration.
No doubt, you are great in heart and mind.
That's why you give me clarion calls
on every celebration, again and again.
Your highness energises me to pen this poem;
describing my inner feelings on receiving
your blessings that further inspire my soul
to dedicate the same to your holy feet.

Your Excellency!
Please do not deprive me of availing myself
the chance of offering my prayer to you,
as I am one of your loyal devotees.

03 March, 2019

An Ultimate Directive

The presence of your excellencies are
spread all over the world, and you move
freely everywhere, my dear Nature!
The revelation of your existence manifests
now and then in many versatilities.
There are billions of admirers of your amazing
qualities, but all are not able to recognise, or,
give proper importance to your excellence,
there remain many examples.

But, your Excellency! Never did I become
a victim of any kind of misapprehension;
even though you appear before me without any
prior information or, in disguise of any
other form beyond my identification.
Sometimes you appear merely like a beggar;
in disguise of the pale and dry Summer.
Sometimes, like a kind lady presenting the pitcher,
full of water, like the Monsoon, the lifesaver.
Sometimes you appear like the holy mother—
'Autumnal Queen'; directly from heaven,
along with your all family members.
Sometimes you create a sensation on tiny leaves

of gooseberry trees during the winter breeze.
Sometimes, even to rejuvenate every living cell
on the Earth during Spring.

Apart from your all efforts, always you keep me
awakened to make me a vigilant watchman.
Only to check my efficiency levels and capacity
to find out and detect any of your planned
slackness or freakishness.
My time-tested experience immediately notices
your deceitful negligence, if any.
Even though you have, so far, kept it secret
to your heart on the probable date of my retirement
and to make me free from all these responsibilities.

Now, I am waiting for that sacred moment—
when I would be fortunate enough to receive
a long-awaited directive from you
in order to attain ultimate salvation, the only
the desired destination for every human being!

11 March, 2019

Cuckoo—My Inspirer

For a long time, I am bereaved by my parents
and passing through the phase of misfortunes.

My dear Cuckoo!
Every year during the Spring, you appear
before me as one of my kind-hearted well-wisher
carrying abandoned love and affection
to console me in the moment of my distress.
You do not appear alone; rather accompanied with
fairy flower; 'Bastard', known as 'fire of the forest',
along with many more friends, including
the romantic flow of southern breezy air.

Oh, the bird, close to my heart!
How I can cordially welcome you all
as I do not have adequate resources and facilities
at my meagre setup, although you, in disguise,
guide me as the protector!
The musical tune of your singings reflects great power
of hypnotism that provides me a healing touch full of
love and care; also leads me to forget all my miseries
during the period of your gracious presence.
You awake me in the morning while singing

in your inherent musical tune.
Again in the evening, you sing to lull me.
During the day you plan how to energise my mind
and encourage me to overcome my shortcomings,
apart from teaching me the lessons—
Feelings of happiness in life are short-lived,
but feelings of miseries remain in the mind forever
as a memory that is unforgettable.

I shall never forget your lesson—
A problem in life is not solved automatically
just by keeping an eye closed on that,
rather, by that time, it multiplies many folds.
I consider myself lucky to get your favour.
I bow my head to pay my whole-hearted respect
to great Nature, whom I consider as 'Supreme'.
I believe in his noble directives.
Every Spring you appear before me, enabling me
to regain aspiration.

21 March, 2019

I am that Coward Poet

I am that coward poet still living on this Earth,
enjoying goodwill as a dignified person in society.
Having that view in my mind I regularly
attend gatherings and seminars to focus my image
and grab praises and applause.

Today even I can recall that event:
the old episode of the famous epic 'Ramayana'.
Several hundred years ago I was also present
on an auspicious occasion of the crowning ceremony
of prince 'Rama' as king of 'Ayodhya';
and his beloved wife 'Sita' as queen,
who had jointly returned to the capital
after a long gap of a decade in exile.
On that occasion, I also joined the public agitation
while shouting the slogan—
Before she acceded the throne,
Sita had to pass the ordeal by holy 'Fire'
to prove her modesty as she might have lost her
'chastity' during her long captivity in enemy territory.

I, the coward poet, knowingly, overlooked
the prevailing social system, the 'patriarchy' in vogue.

It was the foremost duty of the husband to protect
the modesty of his wife as he had to lead
dominating role in managing his family affair.
Instead of voicing against this dominating
century-old 'patriarchy' system, I, as a poet
authored volumes of chapters on the same epic:
which had ultimately been recognised as a
marvellous literary creation, ages after ages.

Even nowadays, female devotees
in some sections of society are not permitted to enter
the place of worship of their faiths to offer prayers.
My cowardly mind prefers to maintain silence,
and as a poet follows the route of opportunism.
I conceptualise and write election manifestos and
slogans on behalf of the leaders of political parties;
bearing a silent hope that I may bag felicitations.
Therefore, I am reluctant to raise my finger
against any political decision that may act
against the interest of the masses ultimately.

I fail to assess the credibility of those leaders.

While following this process I express my inability
of acquiring the power of proper judgement.
But my mind from within claims myself
as a responsible judge in a court of law.
In this process, my mind ultimately feels confused
and cheated by following its own tactics.

I repent. I am the same devious and poltroon poet.
Without assessing my indigenous acumen
and proper powers of self-assessment, I participate
in seminars to grab praises from the audience;
but try to be reluctant to self-criticism.

27 March, 2019

Pursuit for Perfection

By virtue of their whole-hearted love and care,
all my near and dear and well-wishers
have always guided me in a positive direction—
To obtain mental satisfaction as a
career-aspirant of a poet or painter; it is pertinent
for one to become polite and gentle in behaviour.
Furthermore, one has to love the vast nature
irrespective of any border, around the world.

My dear respectable well-wishers!
You have taught me many more—
To be acquainted with the ever-changing pattern
of vibrant seasons and also to witness
the boundless beauty of the sky.
Similarly, it is equally important to know
the behaviour of all living beings of this world,
even at a remote and virgin corner.
And to keep pace with their pulse, habits,
including their liking and disliking.

Oh, my loving well-wishers!
You have further taught me the lessons—
To achieve credibility as a poet or painter

in a true sense, one has to be sensible enough,
and above all, to be a humanitarian.
As Samaritan, one should come forward
to initiate positive steps to reduce suffering
of the people in distress.

Side by side, you have also cautioned me—
To be vigilant and mentally prepared thereon;
to face the consequences like hostile criticism,
threats and even the ultimatum.
Side by side; no doubt, one has to be a protestant
by virtue of conscious mind against the un-ethics
prevalent in society following the barriers of castes,
creeds and faiths, beyond geographic borders.

I would like to evaluate my inherent calibre
to find the paragon of perfection as an aspirant
of a budding poet or painter.

28 March, 2019

The Mystique Magician

Early dawn, while welcoming the day,
I feel amazed to see the vast nature around me
flooded with enchanting lights all over.
With this mystic and unique illumination,
I feel impressed and lose my self-control.

I ask my queries—
Does anyone know the charismatic and
mystic magician who bears the magnificent-tricks
to illuminate every part of this vast world
every day at regular intervals?
Does anyone know his or her address?
And can I pay a visit to that destination as
the human step has already placed its marks
on another planet?

To console my impatient mind,
everyone replies on the same line—
Although, we, the human beings on this Earth
claim ourselves as the most powerful and supreme
amongst all living beings in the Universe;
but it is hellish with all the nonsense!
In fact, the great Sun, Moon, and the Stars

moving in the Universe since time immemorial
have not yet been able to find out the answer; as to where
they have got a magnificent source of energy from
and who the mystic magician is to bless them
always, without any lapse, even for a moment!

05 April, 2019
Rohini, New Delhi

The Son of the Soil

I feel proud to be a son of the Soil.
But, very often I repent from within
for not having a sense of belonging.

Mother 'Soil', the dearest!
Today even I do remember that very day;
back to nearly four decades, when I abandoned
your affectionate care for the sake of my career
and to earn bread and butter for my dependents.

At the moment of my departure; drops of tears
from your swollen eyes came down the cheeks.
The drops of tears ultimately got accumulated
throughout the decades; thereby raising the level
of the nearby water bodies, and also wetlands.

Flocks of geese and ducks; while swimming
used to ask about my welfare and whereabouts.
You maintained uneasy silence, but you didn't
forget to communicate their sentiments to me.
But I hardly cared to respond.

My dear mother 'Soil'!
To my surprise, coming back to your love and
affectionate arms nearly after four decades, now
I notice major changes in your style of behaviour,
and even your facial appearance.
I do not find the presence of those water bodies.
I miss those delightful swimming flock of birds,
their chorus while returning to the night shelters.
Those water bodies no longer exist as these are
filled up and occupied by multistoried buildings.

But alas! Oh, my dear mother 'Soil'!
The residents of the multistoried complex have even
changed the name and identity which was given
by the ancestors centuries earlier.
How I can address you with a different name!

03 May, 2019

Assaults to the Modest Moon

Oh, my dear 'Chandrayan Second'!
Although you are uninvited, I am delighted
by your vibrant presence on my pale surface.

You know very well; I am regarded as the most
enchanting planet on this orbit, moving alone
around the Sun, far from your source of origin,
beyond the formation of the calendar — the 'Time'.
I am moving around the Sun without interference
of any other planet in the vast space of the Universe.

Perhaps, it is one of the reasons of human beings
on the Earth are attracted to me since their childhood.
One after the other, their attempts to step in here
began early seven decades of the last century onward.
And, it is regularly continued without any rest.
Thereafter, without even obtaining my permission,
the soil-sample from this surface was taken away
by men for the purpose of study, and the specimen
was displayed as their glorious achievement.

Oh, my dear 'Chandrayan Second'!
Very recently you have been deputed here

with a noble mission of discovery or invention.
In fact, like a rude rampant, you are peeing into
my virginity to distort my natural modesty, as the
the human community has already done the same
in their planet, the Earth, repeatedly.
The ultimate objective of these ventures is mainly
to exploit the natural recourses of this planet.

Oh, the human inhabitants of the Earth!
Kindly take it for granted. Your achievement of
exploration will not only pave the way for the
destruction
of human civilisation on Earth but also destabilise
other planets of the Universe. It is a warning.
The time is not far behind unless you change
your mind as early as possible!

22 July, 2019

Sun's Grace on Your Face

While sitting quietly in a corner of a mini-balcony;
covered with iron railings of my modest dwelling,
again and again, I look high beyond the greenery
to see your juvenile and charming beauty.
The vibrant vermilion line on your forehead
reminds me of the brilliance of the radiant Sun.
The vision of my poetic mind tries to bring down
the sunny vermilion line from your shining forehead
to the flowing waves of the river Ganges.
While taking a holy bath in the Ganges
I feel your feminine vibrancy and juvenility,
that reminds me of the blooming beauty
of a lotus flower flows adrift for the salvation
towards a boundless ocean, and I feel scared!
But during the dusk, the gracious vermilion line
on your forehead turns towards me and ensures—
Don't be bewildered after the sunset.
Now not the Sun, but the graceful Moon will
appear on this forehead to illuminate the Earth.
The twinkling stars smilingly address their queries—
Whether the elegant sky and the Moon will
now be associated themselves in the courtship
and both will embrace each other!

The Earth, down the line, anxiously waits for a
probable birth of an innocent star in the Universe!

31 July, 2019

The Afflicted Earth

The great Earth always desires to be amiable,
flexible, and generous to all the life-beings.
She is ready to change her strategy from time to time,
as per the necessity of her affectionate life-beings.
But self-propagated human races forbid her.

Kind-hearted, afflicted Earth tends to be liberal.
But human races are mostly greedy and
try to snatch and rob her bounty of treasures.
The magnificent and charismatic Earth desires
to offer her hidden confidentiality of charms
for the improvement of human behaviour.
But their shrewd temperament and the
manner of dealings compels her to be impatient.
Ultimately she finds no other alternative
but to invite pandemic diseases, severe disasters
and calamity, without giving any prior warning.

With a great expectation to rectify and uplift
the mental status of human beings,
she mobilises the divine incarnation of holy disciples
and priests, from time to time.

So that; the level of doctrine may induce nobleness
in the human genes, generation after generation.

But alas! After the demise of individual holy souls;
their so-called trusted followers do not maintain
that orders, status, and ethics, instead they put their
own interest and attention towards establishing his
or her position among the followers,
thereby hampering the established social harmony.
As a result, the Earth feels scared and insecure.

Prince 'Sidharth' denounced his legitimate claim
on the throne and proceeded for self-meditation.
He became 'Buddha' on attaining enlightenment.
He preached lifelong for humanity—
    'Only love and fraternity can
    win over malice and hatred.'
It is ironic that day by day this noble concept
is being diluted and on the pretext of peace and
progress of human society, secret plans are being
mobilised in the labs to destabilise the existence
of the Earth!

Afflicted Earth feels jerked, as her lifelong effort
has turned to be futile, and now what's the way out
for her survival?

03 September, 2019

'Bapu'—In My Dream...

At the end of a busy day of an elegant
Autumn night, I went to the bed late,
and I was in deep sleep.
Meanwhile, to my pleasant surprise, 'Gandhi-Ji',
the 'Father of the Nation', our beloved 'Bapu',
appeared in my dream very silently.
Touching my temple affectionately,
he asked me quietly— "Hey, my dear!
After the independence of this country;
leaving me alone, how are you guys pulling-on
for the last many decades in a divided India?"

He continued— "Honestly speaking,
as I was abandoned by my fellow countrymen,
even leaving aside from the soil of my origin,
I have been continuously fluttering and wandering
hither and thither without anyone noticing or caring."

With due respect and most obediently,
I touched his feet and embraced him emotionally.
He was standing before me in the same leaning pose
on a stick; wearing a white cotton 'dhoti', covering
only the middle half of his lean and slim body.

But in the dim light all over the room; I noticed
that the patches of blood stains on his white attire
were still visible, though with time
for several decades, the patches had turned
into a dull blackish brown.

To avoid any adverse and awkward situation,
I quickly spread the hand-woven mat on the floor
for his sitting arrangement to get him relaxed
a little, as he was looking very tired and disgraced.
By this time, I was feeling consoled and
fortunate enough, my mind became emotional
while thinking even for a moment that, it was the
the first occasion I could see him face to face
in my lifetime, though not in reality, but in a dream.
So what! My memory started running faster
towards the past, back several decades.

Otherwise, in reality, we the countrymen and
the entire world lost his physical presence
long ago since the year Nineteenth-Forty-Eight,
when I was merely a child of four,
and ignorant of his remarkable contribution
towards the upliftment of the downtrodden
and untouchables in human society
and to make this country free.
Like a motion picture, the tragic sequence of his
assassination started screening in my mind.

Though the heart-boiling tragic incident had
taken place at a faraway place from my home town,
but in reality, today even vividly I remember
the funeral that was arranged by thousands
of grief-stricken people in our suburban town,
on an open ground of our then native village,
to pay homage to the departed soul of their
beloved, 'Bapu', the 'Mahatma Gandhi'.

In the end; mourning villagers, irrespective of
any age, caste, creed, and faith, carried
many of Bapu's elegant portraits, hand in hand.
They proceeded in procession towards the bank
of rivulet 'Chitra', and sailed on rows of boats,
following one after another, to the confluence
of river 'Padma' alias 'Ganges', flowing to the
ocean 'Bay of Bengal', for immersion of those
photos and portraits of their adorable
'Bapu', in order to attain ultimate salvation
of the great soul, 'Mahatma Gandhi'.

Getting 'Bapu' so close, sitting comfortably
on the mat, my suppressed tender sentiment
got provoked to share those touchy incidents
with him, but my conscious mind immediately
overpowered me and decided not to divulge
those memorable yet historical facts to the
highly respectable guest.

However; I was feeling highly fortunate
and honoured to receive such a great personality
as a guest at my shabby shelter.
But my septuagenarian mind was curious enough
to know the reason for his kind appearance,
after so many years of absence.
Further, leaving aside all these eventualities,
and to quench my curiosity, I was about to ask him
the question casually to know the main purpose
of his appearance during October,
the month of his birth anniversary, which was
about to approach very shortly, only after this
midnight would be over silently.

My presence of mind reacted quickly and uttered
politely— "Beloved 'Bapu'! Nowadays;
at this crucial juncture, we the common people
of this great Nation, and the continent as well,
are missing your presence and valuable guidance."

While responding to my query, he replied gently,
—"My dear! I am too feeling monotonous.
After so many years of achieving independence
of this country; hardly anyone recognises me
in their daily life, nowadays.

Faintly I remember, that fateful evening
of 30th January 1948, to follow my routine
with a holy mind, along with other companions,

I was walking towards the prayer-hall, to perform
the evening prayer, in the capital of New Delhi."

He continued,
— "That winter evening, without my knowledge,
all of a sudden I got a bullet in my chest, and
immediately lost my consciousness forever.
Since then, only my soul is moving around,
from door to door of my beloveds.
But, it was irony that, most of them who were
acquainted with me refused to recognise me
anymore, and preferred to keep a safe distance.
My dear! By this time, they had also gone to their
much desired attainment, the ultimate salvation."

Obediently I refused to accept his logic,
and replied,
—"Bapu! Excuse me, please.
Irrespective of rich and poor; almost every citizen
of this Nation, carries your remembrance
in their heart and mind, as well as in their purses.
For your kind information, your smiling face is printed
prominently on currency notes of different values.
Perhaps, you have noticed, your portraits, statues
and photographs in different postures are installed
at several important sites within the country and
beyond, and even at places you had not visited
during your lifetime."

"You may feel consoled to get the information
that, the common people of this country,
various organisations, as well as the governments
of the States and at the Centre, have decided
to celebrate your one hundred and fiftieth
birth anniversary throughout this year,
as a mark of respect to the devotion and the
sacrifice of your life for the sake of common people
and achieving freedom of our country and this
subcontinent as a whole."

His loose lips, under unruly moustache uttered
mildly, — "Dear! They are installing my statues
and portraits depicting my body postures only,
but overlooking the very philosophy, idealism and
sacrifice that I had practised throughout my life,
till my last breath!"

In a sarcastic tone, 'Bapu' quickly reacted,
—"Yes! I have also been briefed that, instead of
implementing and highlighting the ideology of
those prominent leaders into reality, only their
statues are now being installed at a magnificent height
to undermine even the image of the vibrant sunlight,
as it has recently been erected on the bed of the river
Narmada, near Sardar-Sarovar-Dam, with a main
objective of developing interest for the tourists."

Listening to him, and sensing his touchy sentiment
on this point, quietly I begged to offer,
— "Bapu! I feel confused about your thinking.
We all knew the situations of that time.
At that crucial juncture, when you were moving
from door to door, around the riot-torn society
in different parts of this country to restore normalcy
and to bring back peace and age-old amity
among the citizens of different faiths, and you were
even fasting for an indefinite period, in order to
serve the purpose, at that crucial moment
your trustworthy followers, instead of extending
their ideological supports and physical presence
to your side, they were busy delivering speeches
with the historical headline —'Tryst With Destiny'
at the Parliament in Delhi, and also in planning
for hoisting the flag of independence from the
historical compound of 'Red Fort' in the capital city
of newly formed country, leaving aside a major part
of a united territory of our original motherland."

And in response to my briefings, he said,
— "My dear! Again you are intelligently
trying to divert me from my basic queries."

Politely, I apologised and reacted, "I am sorry!
Let me brief you about the present condition
of our great Nation, and its millions of citizens.
I hope you will not mind listening to a few words

on the present condition of our family.
In the year Nineteen Forty-Seven, when
the long-awaited independence was declared
after dividing one Nation into two, I was merely
a child of four, as I have told you before.
No doubt, my condition was worse than yours.

Perhaps you were aware of the fact that,
my ancestors, along with their siblings had to
abandon their original family roots unwillingly.
By force, they had to adapt themselves as refugees.
Without prior knowledge of their close neighbours,
they had to flee, along with me, the boundary
and the check-post of a newly formed country
in the darkness of midnight to escape death.
Since my childhood, I have been moving
from place to place with an expectation of
settling down at a permanent address but in vain.

Bapu! It is ironic that to date
I am identified as a refugee.
A ruling government in a democratic country
is changing and I am being asked to submit
proof of identity as a domicile of this country,
though the original country was divided into two
on the volatile basis of religious beliefs and faiths."
I continued, —"Bapu! At that time,
as I understand, you were overruled and sidelined
by the dominating and powerful ruler, who believed

the basic political ideology —'Divide and Rule'.
And this ideology was indirectly supported by the
power-crazy young indigenous followers, who were
ambitious about their careers, rather than
maintaining the integrity and unity of this
great Nation and to serve its citizens.
Had you been bold enough with your oratory power
as an expert legal professional to overrule their idea,
I would have not been a refugee in my own country.

Bapu! Please excuse my audacity.
No doubt, it was a pitiable act to assassinate an
adorable personality like you who had devoted
his whole life for the downtrodden.

I would like to tell you about the act of the assassin.
Had he been a nationalist in the true sense, either he,
or supporters would have initiated countrywide
political movements against the decision on baneful
bifurcation of the motherland and to resist the proposal
under any circumstances, instead of killing an elderly
and lonely person of your status, who had
not even asked for a security guard for self-protection
during his entire political life.

As an after-effect of the political movement, perhaps
the ruler would have been forced to reconsider
and withdraw that harmful policy of bifurcation,
in order to settle the dispute more favourably and

sympathetically, without playing ducks and drakes against the life of millions of common citizens and the Nation at large."

For a moment Bapu touched his bony chest with his right hand, perhaps, to feel the palpitation!

Again I continued— "Bapu! Perhaps you are aware of the fact that; one integrated country of that time is now divided into three, on the basis of different faiths, ideologies, races, as well as spoken languages. One by one wars, seize-fires, cross-border firings, terrorisms, killings of innocent citizens on both side all along the border areas, have lost news value, since these are the facts, and are being considered routine.

—Bapu! Will the sacred soil of this country be able to originate a mass revolution to unite these three divided parts into one Nation, as it was earlier, following the example of the Germans, who had set an example of patriotism in world history during the year Nineteen Ninety?
Or, to produce gems of leaders, who would be able to organise the movement to serve this objective?
Excuse me please; like many other ordinary citizens of this country, I am also an optimist!"

—"Bapu! History admits that you had lifelong sincerely promoted autonomy of 'self-reliance',

without having any disparity between the followers
of different religious faiths and beliefs, language,
castes, colours, and creeds.
You were determined to uphold the equal status
for the downtrodden, but perhaps
nowadays, it is also being manipulated under
the cover of different rules and regulations.
And cast-related classism is still being followed
altogether in different manners and forms.

Instead of promoting the status
of equality in our society, we are indulging
disturbances and tension between ourselves.
How long will these types of political games
of creating differences between domiciled people;
under the banner of development of a particular area
or region in this country, be continued ultimately
to disintegrate the original bond of the society?

Nowadays the trend is an open secret that
in order to earn individual image and to grab power;
the local leaders are originating different issues and
organising state-wise strikes and forcing the closer
of productive units in a state, thereby, paralysing
country's economy as a whole, to compel and force
the union government to divide one state and
form many more in the name of paving
the way for efficient administration.

Hardly any leader talks on vital issues—
like curbing the uncontrolled population.
Rather; the slogans of fanaticism are being
indulged to create boundaries on the basis of
citizens' mother tongue and spoken languages.
No one even cares, although we have become free
and independent, we are not at all free from dangers
from our immediate neighbours beyond the borders.
Hope; you can, very well, sense my anticipation."

Participating in a long discussion with him;
I gathered the courage to represent my personal views,
— "Bapu! I feel that all religious faiths regulate our
souls.
Similarly, the political ideologies regulate our minds.
But both, individually and independently move
within the separate and specific abstract periphery.
None of them should ever interfere with each other.
Neither the faith nor the politics should overpower,
or interchange each other's positions.
Otherwise; there are possibilities of prevailing
unruly and chaotic conditions in human society.
And unfortunately, we the general public become
prey very often to that type of interference mostly."

Listening to me patiently, 'Bapu' raised a few lines
of wrinkles on his forehead, and gently replied,
— "My dear boy!
Hope; you have not yet forgotten the historical facts.

Nearly three hundred years ago; keeping aside his
original habitat secured, a lion, the king of the jungle,
covering a long distance of several thousand miles
of navigation on sea and river, reached the shore
of a remote Indian coastal territory
on the bank of the Bay of Bengal.

At that time, you know the fact that
the vast and virgin land of this Subcontinent
was enriched with untapped natural resources.
It was divided into so many states, and those parts,
on several occasions, were invaded and being ruled
by different races and families, who proclaimed
themselves with many titles like Rajas, Maharajas,
Sultans, Lodi, Sahen-Shahs, Kings, and Emperors.
And those rulers, instead of looking after the welfare
of their subjects, were mainly engaged in fighting
against each other to expand their territory
and fulfil their interests.

At an opportune moment, the witty lion
exhorted to utilise the situation in his favour.
Grabbing the territory, one after the other,
and got into their fold of ruling, as one Nation
throughout the Eastern Subcontinent.
The lion, with his forces, ruled over this region
over a couple of centuries, and ultimately he was
compelled to abandon this territory unwillingly,

masterminding the divide of this territory
based on religious faiths.

It was ironic that the witty lion again divided
this integrated kingdom into two on the basis of
religion and faith, and our so-called popular leaders,
failed to understand the cleverness of his policy—
'Divide and Rule', and they were greedy enough
to grab the portfolios and the illuminative posts."

Bapu continued,
"But, my dear! We must be careful and
alert to keep our territory safe and secure.
Otherwise it will be difficult to drive out other
greedy and fierce wild animals like leopards, bears,
and dragons as they move very close to our border
just beyond the ocean and hilly areas.
We all know, according to historical records,
that our territory had been invaded and ruled over
several times in the past by outside powers.
I feel sorry to say, nobody looks into that angle."

At this moment, earnestly I appealed to him,
— "Bapu! Although unfortunately, you were
assassinated by an individual; perhaps due to few
ideological differences, but people of the whole Nation,
feel grieved and shocked even today,
and irrespective of age, respect you from their heart.
Why don't you appear again to your loving Nation

to provide proper guidance to the custodians
of the present generation!"

Bapu, taking a long breath, replies in a pensive mood,
— "My dear! I am not aware of the fact whether the
concept of ideological differences still exists, or not.

With the pace of Time, political situations
worldwide have changed a lot.
Similarly, the mind of the general public
and the leaders, who are, at present, in power,
have also changed in a big way.
My conscious mind does not permit me
to become the 'Father of the Nation' once again."

To my shocking surprise; suddenly I realised,
our beloved 'Bapu' silently disappeared.

02 October, 2019

The Birthday—Mirror

Every year, on the date Sixteenth of November
appears to me as a splendid mirror, although
the dawn of every day seems to be a boon
from the mighty and fabulous infinity for me—
an elderly septuagenarian.

Every year, one after the other, I have not only
become older, but also turned to be a lucky owner
of huge treasures with blessings from my elders,
praiseworthy greetings from well-wishers
and associates on these occasions.

I do not even know how to express my obligation,
or reciprocate to their noble gestures who had taken
every possible care to bring me up from the date
of my birth on this Earth, and to guide me always
ignoring their well-being till their last breath.
By this time, they all have left this earthy-soil
to attain the ultimate salvation of their departed souls.
I bow my head with full respect for their memories.

Still, I cherish their fond associations while
they arranged my naming ceremony in my infancy,

even managing the sacrament-function
of my first lesson on the holy day of worshipping
'Debi-Sarswati', the 'Goddess of Learning'.
Indeed it was a stepping-stone to building my fortune.

Nevertheless, I have come across a long journey
through experiencing several happy and joyous
moments; coupled with sufferings due to tragic and
untimely departures of my affectionate beloveds.
Unwillingly I have become part and parcel of the game
'topsy-turvy' between two prominent contestants—
'Time', the great, and 'Life', the most delicate!

From the core of my heart, I do pay my regards
to the great felicitators— Infinitive Sky,
the amiable green Nature, the humble breezy air,
the affluent water reserves, fabulous land-masses
and all life-beings including human races.

But none of them has ever asked for any kind of
return in any manner in lieu of services rendered
by them for bringing me up.
They all know very well— I am meagre a person
and incapable of any return, I'm only a recipient.

In the evening, earnestly I appeal to my conscience
to understand— the blessings; whatever I have been
bestowed on, time to time, are fabulous in quantum
and precious enough in every manner.

I am not at all competent enough to get these favours.
I feel fortunate not to lose them in disdain.

Above all, I should feel complacent
and grateful to the mighty and magnanimous,
yet invisible infinity till my last breath.

16 November, 2019

The Moment of the Last Judgement

Since my birth on this Earth
I have, no doubt, been fortunate enough
to be granted fabulous grants and favours
always by the great well-wishers, who are
not visible even for a moment.

But, during the long span of my life,
not even for a single moment has my coward
and ungrateful mind ever expressed
a minimum sense of gratitude towards the kindness
bestowed on me by the beloved well-wishers.
Not even for a single moment I have evaluated
whether as a human being, I have ever been
entrusted any responsibilities to be attended
for the society that bears all the odds for me.

My fugitive mind has always misguided me to be
aberrant towards the tantalisation of the immoral.
My careless and ungrateful mind has never
thought of any plan and proceedings —
as to what is the right manner to return
fabulous grants and favours that I have been

receiving from my beloved well-wishers.
And what is the process to be followed
for proper regularisation.

Now, I am on the verge of retirement
and ready to say goodbye to my beloved life,
as everybody's lifespan has a definite limitation.
From the core of my heart, I regard the universal truth —
At the time of final judgement, no explanation,
nor any excuse in any manner would be
considered valid in the court of Supreme Judge.
Even; there will not be any point of relief
on the clause of 'Benefit of Doubt'.
Furthermore, as the rebirth of life in this Nature
is absurd, and no such concept on
compassionate-ground is considered favourable.

Time and again I have failed to convince
my adamant mind to realise the 'Truth of Life'.

14 March, 2020

Address of the Heaven

As I believe in my mind; no one knows—
Where and how to find the grace of divine God.
No one even knows the direction of heaven,
and where He is gracefully embellished.
Further, no one knows the address of the hell,
where the shrewd demon lives and remains
busy always in implementing evil plans.

No one perhaps contradicts; as I have realised—
Both the divine God and the shrewd demon are
cherished in the human mind and soul, side by side.

The human mind, through the type of activities;
expresses the charismatic presence of holy God;
or, the heinous behaviour of the shrewd demon.
But every human mind acts a double role.
And both of them wait for the opportunity
to come out of the brain to furnish their role;
either to be worshipped or to be punished.

Once one of my best friends robbed me
of my important and precious documents.
At an appropriate time; I appealed to him—

My dear! Neither do I wish to prove your offence
in any court of law, nor, to become the judge
to punish you for your deliberate offence.
Instead, I earnestly request your mind to act
as a holy God, but not as a notorious Demon.
Ultimately, you will be surprised to discover
that your mind and soul have turned
to a holy place automatically, like heaven.

20 March, 2020
(Four criminals, out of six, have been hanged
in Tihar Jail, New Delhi, today for their crime of
raping a young lady, namely 'Nirbhaya' and injuring
her brutally that caused her death in the year 2012.)

The Spring in Quarantine

Receiving an advance information
from Spring; the king of all seasons,
the flowering plants— 'Cotton-silk' and 'Bastard'
have been delighted in their heart and mind.
    On arrival of the Spring, they will bloom in
    a festive and colourful mood all over nature.
    The whole world is anxiously waiting to
    witness that elegant and auspicious exposure.
    My mind is equally inspired and flying high
    like a bird, and remains busy in discussion
    on various topics of high esteem.
Meanwhile the Spring; accompanied with an
unknown face-'Covid-19', appears suddenly;
not in a joyous mood, but in morose-look
carrying tragic news that, breaking out of this
contagious disease and pandemic death alarms,
determining the disaster throughout the world.
    Human society is confused and scared
    for not having any knowledge about the
    way out for prevention, since proper care
    and medical advice is yet known to none.
Finding no other immediate ways of remedial steps;
though the 'lock-down' process has been imposed

to cordon human mobility, but the world economy
will plunge rapidly into the deep sea, thereby, dictating
the process of ultimate death, instead of revival.
This process will reassess the definition of the
'Developed' and 'Developing Nations',
probably to set up a new equation worldwide.
 The tragic phenomenon of Second 'World War'
 is still blowing in the air, and yet 'Covid-19'
 defeats the velocity of those tragic memories.
 Human society neither welcomes nor appreciates
 any such blessing or kindness of 'Covid-19'.
Rather, nature worldwide desires—
Let the Spring appear with the blessings of all
colourful festivals, in every corner, one by one.
Let the spring bird 'Koel' sing in a melodious tune.

20 March, 2020
(The poem is dedicated to the
victims of 'Covid-19' worldwide)

My Adorable Supreme

With whole-hearted regards; everyone affirms—
You possess amazing aesthetic beauty
without having a minor point of unpleasant aspect.
Further, you have fabulous reserves
of five varieties of wealthy and powerful resources,
mainly the Soil-Water-Fire-Air and vast Space
to regulate the Universe.
Even then, I bear a sincere desire to further illustrate
your inner beauty in my way.
Immediately my mind feels depressed to realise
the fact that I have meagre talent and resources
to do so with proper dignity.

With my limitation; I am unable to describe
your incredible images and boundless beauty
in different seasons all through the year.
To follow your silent directives;
some varieties of foliage bloom in different seasons
and some bloom in all seasons throughout the year.
Therefore; you provide a suitable climate,
as well as, the weather in their favour.
Similarly, you are following the same ethics
for different varieties of fruits and vegetables.

Thereby you maintain the variety of beauty
to avoid the monotony of the system all over.

Oh nature, my adorable Supreme!
During the Spring; with your motherly touch
you embellish the greeneries in different colours
to attract curious butterflies towards the flowers
of different varieties.
The groups of cuckoos having been impressed
by your elegant beauties sing in a melodious tune
to pay respect towards your divine role.
Even the essence of newly grown mango-spikes
attracts the swarm of honeybees.
I am amazed to listen to their humming sound,
that predicts in advance about timely arrival
of juicy fruits in the coming Summer season.
Apart from all these, notional goodwill and
happiness along with heart-breaking distresses
and sufferings knock my worn-out dwelling
without any prior notice, one after another.

In due course of the ensuing Summer season;
the hot spell extends its support to the
mustard field and the shaded 'Amaltas' trees
to bloom and turn yellow to please the Sun.

Flaunting clouds in Monsoon bring delights
and freshness all over the atmosphere
to welcome the shower of raindrops.

Sparking lightning illuminates the sky and
the horizon with a thundering sound, and brings
cheers to all the living beings on the earthy surface.
Heavy showers bring green elevations all over.
My curious mind becomes spellbound
and witnesses your splendid beauty.
The group of joyous peacocks and peahens
in usual dancing rhythm extend their
festive companionship to me cordially.

During Autumn, the southern breeze carries
delightful essence of 'Night Jasmine', and
gently brings the cheerfulness of the festive season
to every household.
The tips of the meadow grass already grown
in the green field hold dewdrops lovingly
throughout the night to welcome the tender
sunlight of the next early morning.
On the magical touch of tender sunlight;
the dewdrops spark like diamonds in multiple
to enhance your autumnal beauty.

On arrival of the Winter season;
the greedy flocks of birds anxiously wait
on thorny branches of tall 'date' trees to taste
sweetish juices flowing slowly drop by drop
as a natural sequence of a yearly phenomenon.

The darkness of the new-moon night draws
the collyrium on your widened eyelids.
The gorgeous full-moon shines on your forehead.
You are amazingly beautiful in all respect.

Oh, gorgeous Nature, my adorable Supreme!
I do not dare to apply my minor brush-work
even for a little, since I am holding barely
an empty bracket, without having any asset on it.
Please bless me a little from your vast reserves,
so that, I shall be able to devote and offer them
again to your holy feet in the form of your praises,
as I sincerely believe—
You are my adorable Supreme!

23 March, 2020

Compassion of the 'Corona-virus'

Earth and Nature— both are twin sisters,
trusted and always sympathetic to each other,
since the auspicious moment of their formation.
Even then, they feel threatened by the rude and
exploitative behaviour of their most smart and
talented children, mainly human beings who are
brought up under their affectionate and motherly care.

In comparison to other children on this planet,
their avaricious and exploitative activities
are even being initiated to claim their control
on other planets and stars of the Universe.
Further, the unplanned growth of the
human population is causing pressure on both,
Earth and Nature to manage the global system.

Earth and Nature—both are confused;
how to save their own identity and existence!
With great hope for their survival; both the twins
invite 'Corona-virus', for quick pandemic action.
It is the repetition of age-old philosophic and
religious prophecy as depicted in 'Geeta'—
"For repression of evils and protection of

righteousness; the 'Holy-Soul' incarnates
on the Earth's surface from time to time."
And 'Corona' as a rescuer in the present situation!
As the twin sisters will feel relaxed,
human beings worldwide are scared.

At my age, I am still passing through many such
ups and downs, even pandemic miseries in this life.
I am also compassionate to the feelings of both—
Earth and Nature, including grieving human losses.
If it is considered an offence; and I am sentenced
to death, I shall greatly accept it as an attainment
of my soul's salvation which is the ultimate desire
of every human being.
Even then, let Earth and Nature regain health.
Flocks of birds will sing again hymns of praises
in various tunes to welcome future generations.

27 May, 2020
(Worldwide, 'Corona' has counted the
death of 3,46,000 human lives, to date)

Directives of the Mind

As and when I am grossly inundated
with the memories of my near and dear,
my favourite 'Mind' confidentially advises me—
Not to be emotional out of proportion, as he
discharges his duties as an expert navigator
to guide me and also to look after my welfare.
He is my source of encouragement for each
and every decent goodwill effort.
Equally, he is also a critic of my evil approaches.
On the other hand, he is equally capable of planning
and fabricating conspiracies on my behalf.

He turns to be an honourable judge, even
to scrutinise my offences for conviction,
and to award the punishment to me thereon.
To my surprise; the 'Mind' further explains—
He also suffers for the expiation of my conviction.

No doubt; he is the source of my pleasure,
as well as the miseries in my life so far.
He is the core of purity and impurity both combined.
After all, he inspires me for my rejuvenation.
Lastly, he reflects both— Life and Death.

From his confidential approach; I feel
confused, and try to grapple with the facts of those
old complaints against me, one after another.
With folded hands, I pray to 'Mind' for mercy.

The Mind appears again with his decency.
He turns towards me and advised me to distinguish
the ethics and un-ethics, rights and wrongs.
Instead of setting me free from the allegations,
he confidently declares—
Stupid! To play safe; always try to assess
yourself on a scale of positivity and negativity.
All your offences will accumulate in the
shape of a garland and that will be offered
on your body at the time of your last journey.
At that time, not before me, but you will have to
present yourself, like all others, at the court
of the Supreme Judge for your final judgement.
Though it is bitter to listen, get yourself ready.

30 June, 2020

'Corona'—The Uncrowned King

Darling! For the last several months
you are in my mind and heart always.
Yet, I have missed your physical presence,
due to some conspicuous circumstances
called the 'lock-down', beyond the routine.
In a huff, for long you have not come to me
with your heartfelt compassion and solidarity.
    Perhaps, silently within yourself,
    you have borne those sentiments.
    But, you may not aware of the fact—
    There is one treacherous fellow,
    who is invisible to both of us.
He has been given an identity, Corona-virus.
The virus directs me to fulfil his demands
in every respect; otherwise threatens me
to face dire consequences, thereon.
He refuses to realise my ability or inability,
and is concerned about his self-interest only.
He is eager to count deaths of human lives,
and is not ready to budge even a little.

Pointing his index finger; he threatens—
Abandon your passion for writing poetry,
love, and care for Art and Literature.
He further continues—
Perhaps you are aware of my curses, which are
merely unbearable for human beings.
Refer to the curses of infamous saint-'Durbasa'
of your epic, during the early period-'Treta-yuga'.
Similarly; now I am present here in a new form,
widely known as the virus 'Corona'.
I do not care about the history,
written by human beings.
Even I ignore those eminent personalities,
rulers, namely Genghiz-Khan, Bin-Tughluq,
Timur-Lang, or Nadir-Shah, the plunder
of 'Peacock-Throne'.
I do not care about the geographic boundary
and sovereignty of any country in this world.
I do not even care about the welfare of the
general public, either pious or sinner,
rich or poor, irrespective of colour, caste, creed,
religion and faith, not even leaders, actors,
ministers, kings or queens, and the viceroy.
Though I am not crowned; but a Super king
now ruling over the whole world.
All the ignorant, erudite, orators and

scientists pay their respect to me cordially.
Though my identity is too tiny, not even visible,
I am obviously a life-threatening terror-'Corona',
creator of a new chapter in human history.

26 July, 2020
(To date, nearly Sixteen million people have been affected by this virus, and more than half a million people have lost their lives.)

The Clay or Kiln

In the morning; while walking along with
tender Sunlight, I ask one of the pedestrians,
— Dear! Between the 'Clay' and 'Kiln';
which one is dearer to your heart and mind?
The pedestrian gently replies,
— Sir! I am a farmer. I spend days ploughing
in the field for growing the grains, and thereby
I earn bread and butter for my entire family.
Through this effort, I am able to arrange
thatches to cover my muddy cottage.
Clay or mud is my favourite as it provides me
direct contact with the holy mother Earth.

In the morning; while walking along with the
tender sunlight, I ask the same question to another
person, and diligently he answers my query,
— I am a daily-wage labourer; both are equally dear
to my heart, love is a feeling never comparable.
In exchange for labour, to earn bread and butter
is the main motto of my life.
To me, there is no difference between either
to set up a ridge of the Earth by the edge of a spade,

on agricultural land, or to make bricks out of clay
for the kilns; ultimately to get the fired bricks.

While walking in the morning along with tender
sunlight, I ask the same question to another pedestrian.
The pedestrian smilingly replies in a romantic tone,
— I am a poet and nature-lover, fond of literature.
From time immemorial, the moisture of Earth
helps grow green grasses to cover nature.
The grasses bring cheers to the infant fawns.
The tiny saplings transform into shady trees.
On the branches; flocks of birds sing in rhythms.
They make the nests to welcome their chicks.
Truly, the Earth springs the beats of my heart
every moment and lets the bricks remain aside.

I ask the same question to another pedestrian.
Looking at me, the pedestrian solemnly replies,
— I am a lawyer by profession, and time passes
mostly in court cases through different phases
of legal arguments and counter-arguments.
I believe both the clay and kiln
are in the same rank, without dispute,
as no complaint has, so far, been lodged
in the civil or criminal courts.
According to me, both are equally important
for the progress of society, but the balance
between the two has to be followed judiciously.

In broad daylight, while walking on the road,
I ask the same question to another pedestrian.
He identifies himself as a technocrat-cum-scientist.
Holding a newspaper in hand, he elaborates,
— I spend my days on the tables of laboratories
experimenting with a different scientific thesis.
Therefore; I do not involve myself in these
issues to avoid any further controversies.
Innovation is the ultimate process of attainment
for the supreme, which gives me the satisfaction,
as well as the justification for getting human life.
I am always kin to part with the experimentation.
But, take it for granted that the Earth and Nature
are like the twin sisters of the Mother.
Similarly, the co-existence of the Clay and
the Kiln in a balance is absolutely imperative
to maintain the all-round development of society,
irrespective of any restriction or boundary.
The human body is also the creation of Nature.
Even passing through the different processes,
it attains ultimate salvation to the cordial arms
of the fire or graveyard, thereby, converting
into the Earth.

With my folded hands; respectfully I conclude,
— Oh my dear technocrat-cum-scientist!
Have you ever realised, that the core of knowledge
you possess provokes greedy human behaviour
very often to miss-utilise and divert into the

wrong direction, thereby indulging competition to exploit vast natural resources of this Earth? As the reserves are being merely exhausted, they are targeting other planets under the banner of invention or discovery, thereby, following the old process, —'Might ensures Right'.

Please restrict their wrong intention, otherwise, the day is not far away, when the Sun will lose its powerful glow, and the fate of the Universe will be at stake! Please ask them to realise.

19 August, 2020

Lesson from Nature

The news conveys— A widowed mother;
though both her sons are well-settled
and holding important positions in society,
due to their negligent, unconcerned attitude, and
hostile behaviour, without getting proper care
so far, unfortunately, breathed her last
merely helplessly on a secluded roadside corner.
Nature, the supreme mother, under utter
frustration, tries to evaluate the situation
and realises— always with her affection,
love, and care; she has been bringing all
human beings up, and ultimately they are
behaving in such an inhuman manner
to pay due respect and dutifulness in return
to their nearest superiors and elders!
She decides to teach them a proper lesson
by deputing her reliable assistant 'Covid-19',
and directing drastic action against the offenders.
'Covid' imposes the most severe 'Death' penalty!
Worldwide human community
frightened and trying hard to find
a process to get rid of severe penalties.

Now they have realised a time-tested proverb—
'Action of Nature never dares to any reaction.'
Yet, selfish and greedy human nature forgets
this universal truth and the proverb very often.

23 August, 2020
(Worldwide nearly twenty-three million people are affected by Corona-virus, and over a million people have died so far.)

The Compunctious Cloud

Silently, the Monsoon is disappearing.
The vast sky, at the advent of the Autumn season,
gracefully beckons me early in the morning.
I set my eyes to the sky to find adherent cloud
in different shapes and shades of whitish,
turquoise, and cirrus tones which have given
the sky an elegant and impressive look.
Rays of tender Sun have added beauty all around.
The cloud cheerfully moves in a romantic rhythm
in a different direction to an unknown destination.

Out of curiosity, I address the cloud gently,
— Dear! In my childhood days; both you and I
  had played mischief with our neighbours.
  To surprise me, very often, disguised as rain,
  you embraced me without prior indication.
  Even now, you are capricious and impetuous.
  But, I am bogged down in quarantine due to
  massive outbreak of pandemic 'Covid-19'.

The cloud smilingly questions me,
— Please tell me, how old you are now.
  I have come across the grand climacteric phase

of my life, and after a few years I shall cross
the bar of Septuagenarian, but I am not sure,
whether I shall be privileged to touch my eighties.
Now, please appraise me of your age.

The cloud diligently answers,
— So far, no one has noted the date of my birth.
I am an orphan moving around the space,
and mobile as a refugee, like you. Even
I have no permanent address and destination.

I feel surprised to take note
of how the cloud knows my biodata!
Of course, I am a refugee without any
stable shade above my head.

The cloud further clarifies,
— I possess every detail of every individual
about their credentials, as who has been
driven out from where and when even the
reasons of their evacuation,
who is really responsible for the action.

Merely with a fellow feeling; I ask him again,
— Who are your parents? Are you not aware
of your actual age and date of birth?

The cloud repents,
— I have not been fortunate enough like you.
I have all along been deprived of the affectionate
and loving care of my parents, unlike yours.
Whenever I think about my misfortune;
my sentiments, in form of depression,
turn down into a flow of tears as drops of rain.
I console myself; let the rain, the sign of my
sorrows bring cheers to all the living beings
down the earthy surface.

15 September, 2020

Nature's Partiality

Though I always bow my head to Nature,
seldom do I criticise her for her one-eyed partiality
towards the male genders of her vast kingdom.
With her kind grace; the male gender is given
more physical strength, but not the elegance of
body formations in comparison to the female gender.
As a consequence of inequality; the females are
very often being easy prey to the male's lusts.

In the morning; while reading daily newspapers,
I feel disgusted to look at the various reports
on molestation and cruelty to the female genders.
The news also elaborates on the formal protests and
criticism against these offences, followed by
issuing statements for severe punishment for the
criminals and promising to implement the process
of female-liberalisation by social organisations
and influential groups and individuals.

Elders of the society are judging these offences
and crimes through their veils of
caste, creed, and faith.
Moreover, the legal process to assess the gravity

of the offences, to identify the accused involved,
and to punish the culprits continues for decades.

I understand the reality that
the crimes of cheating-molestation-raping and
murdering are undeterred and never-ending.
These will be continued in society forever.
In order to reduce social crimes; it is time
to initiate reform on human body formation, thereby
establishing equality in the social system all over.

The situation is still cautioning the human society
to find a suitable remedy and solution.
Invention and application of reproductive-techniques
is the latest method of conception.
To maintain equality in the human body:
let us plan to set up a biotechnological laboratory
to create a new genetic method for a new generation
of mankind, which will bear the characteristics of
a hermaphrodite, carrying both male and female genes
in one individual, like 'Ardha-Narishwar',
a combined image of both God and Goddess—
the Lord 'Shiva' and Devi 'Durga' of the Indian epic.

Through this process; an individual body,
at puberty or maturity, will bear the full form of
both the male and female genetic organs.
As a result, perhaps the tendency of sexual abuses
will be minimal, or will virtually be disappeared.

One may be confused to realise the point—
To multiply the future generations; will it
biologically be possible to meet
to fertilise the egg and sperm as both
organs already exist in the same body?

In fact; the example already exists in Nature.
The earthworms have genital organs of both
sexes in their individual bodies.
But, reproduction is possible only by meeting
of the two separate bodies.
Following this process, perhaps, sexual crimes
and brutal killings of innocent victims will be
fewer, and the equality of the human race,
to a great extent, will be established.

23 October, 2020

About the Author

Rudrendra Prasad Ghosh, (born: 16th November, 1944), popularly known as R. P. Ghosh, is simultaneously recognized as an author, painter, poet, sculptor and a nature-lover. To pursue his inherent passion for art and literature; he took early voluntary retirement from a secured and dignified service as 'General Manager' of an undertaking, functioning under the Ministry of Commerce, Government of India, in 2001.

Born on 16th November, 1944, at 'Narail', a suburb town of 'Jessore' district (now in Bangladesh) of undivided India, he became, at an early age, along with his parents and relatives, a refugee, as a victim of the political turmoil which caused the partition of his homeland, while forming two sovereign nations – India and Pakistan in 1947.

Crossing the border between the newly formed nations, his parents and relatives took shelter in a refugee camp, and went from there to a resettlement town at 'Habra' of District North 24- Parganas, near Calcutta (now Kolkata) in independent India.

He obtained his school education initially from local schools, and also from Ramakrishna Mission Vidyapith (Dist-Purulia, West Bengal, India), a chain of educational institutions, being run under philosophic guidance, formulated by Swami Vivekananda, the great philosopher, social- reformer and pioneer of the Indian Renaissance. Thereafter; he graduated in the Art faculty from the Government College of Art, Calcutta in 1968, and started his initial service career in the advertising profession.

He joined 'Nehru Science Centre', under the Ministry of Education and Culture, Government of India, in 1976 at Mumbai. And in 1983, he joined a leading Corporation, under the Ministry of Commerce, Government of India, at New Delhi.

During his long public service career, he visited several countries, i.e. the United Kingdom, France, Soviet Russia

(USSR), Germany (FRG & GDR), Egypt, the UAE and many other countries in the Middle East, number of times.

His creative talents in art and literature reflect his own style of expression, elaborating wide exposures, experiences and interactions with a cross-section of people in societies from different countries and times.

Apart from his drawings, paintings and sculptures, in the literary area, he has authored eleven titles to date. These also include collections of poems and stories in both English and Bengali language.

www.ingramcontent.com/pod-product-compliance
Lightning Source LLC
LaVergne TN
LVHW091108150826
845673LV00002B/743

* 9 7 9 8 8 8 8 0 5 3 7 2 0 *